by Robert Young

P DILLON PRESS, INC.
Minneapolis, Minnesota 55415

For Sara,
who always sticks by me but never sticks to me.

This book is a presentation of Field Publications and Weekly Reader Books. Weekly Reader offers book clubs for children from preschool through high school. For further information write to: **Weekly Reader Books**, 4343 Equity Drive, Columbus, Ohio 43228.

Published by arrangement with Dillon Press, Inc. Weekly Reader is a federally registered trademark of Field Publications.

Cover copyright © 1990 by Field Publications.
Cover photo by Tom Hopkins Studio.

Acknowledgments

Writing this book took a lot of time and work. Luckily, many people helped. I would like to thank: Frank Adam, Dr. William Alexander, Linda Arne, Dr. Marc Binder, Vincent Bonica, Janet S. Byrne, Pam Davis, Alan Dickman, Duane Everard, Joe Forward, Richard Funke, Dr. Richard Gabriel, Bonny Graham, Peter Guerra, Fawn Henderson, Robert Hendrickson, Alice Hoos, Dr. Tom Jefferson, Jim Kyle, Les Levine, Norman Liss, William Nicholson, Barbara Snow, Richard Thomas, Steve Thompson, Bob Webb, Joan Weber, Sara Young, Tyler Young, and my editor Shonagh Dobbs. A special thanks to Ralph Richter of the Warner-Lambert Company and Joan Brunner of the William Wrigley, Jr., Company for their efforts.

Thanks also to the Council On Dental Therapeutics, the Eugene Ballet Company, Fleer Corporation, L.A. Dreyfus Company, Liss Public Relations Incorporated, the Metropolitan Museum of Art, National Aeronautics and Space Administration, Sacred Heart Hospital, Topps Chewing Gum Incorporated, W & F Manufacturing Company, and the William Wrigley, Jr., Company.

Photographs have been reproduced through the courtesy of the William Wrigley, Jr., Company; American Chicle Division, Warner-Lambert Company; Ford Gum and Machine Company, Inc.; Transworld Feature Syndication; Liss Public Relations; and Dr. William Alexander.

Library of Congress Cataloging-in-Publication Data

Young, Robert, 1951-
   The chewing gum book.

   Includes index.
   Summary: Discusses chewing gum, its forms and flavors, its history and technology, and its various uses.
     1. Chewing gum—Juvenile literature. [1. Chewing gum]
I. Title.
TX799.Y68   1989   664'.4   88-31015
ISBN 0-87518-401-4

Dillon Press, Inc., 242 Portland Avenue South
Minneapolis, Minnesota 55415

Printed in the United States of America
1 2 3 4 5 6 7 8 9 10 98 97 96 95 94 93 92 91 90 89

Contents

Bazooka bubble gum rolls off a conveyor belt in the Topps factory.

1 Millions of Mouths Can't Be Wrong

Chewing gum is everywhere.

Do you want to buy some? You're in luck because you can buy it just about anywhere. You can buy it in stores, restaurants, and theaters. You can buy it in stadiums, concert halls, golf courses, and bowling alleys. You can buy it in motel lobbies, service stations, and airports. And then there are machines, thousands of them, located almost everyplace you can imagine. Just drop in some change and out comes your favorite flavor.

Chewing gum has been to every part of the globe and to every nation on the face of the earth. It has been to the highest mountains and the

depths of the oceans. It has been to tiny villages
and crowded cities, to jungles and Antarctica. It
has even been to outer space.

It's everywhere, even some places you wish it
weren't. Look around. It won't take long to find
places where careless people have left chewed
gum. Hardened wads can be found anywhere
people have been, but some places are more
popular than others—sidewalks, wastebaskets,
and under desks and seats of every kind.

Chewing gum is everywhere because people
love to chew it. In the United States alone, people
buy almost two billion dollars worth of chewing
gum in a single year. That's enough chewing gum
for every person of chewing age (over three years
old) to have three hundred pieces. That's almost
one piece every single day of the year for more
than 200 million people!

Why is chewing gum so popular? The answer
is that gum has something for everyone.

Dubble Bubble was one of the first bubble gums in the United States.

Some people like it for its looks. Chewing gum comes in many colors, shapes, and sizes. It also comes in many forms: stick gum, ball gum, bubble gum, tablet gum, liquid-center gum, and candy-coated gum.

Some people like it for its taste. Chewing gum has come in a variety of flavors including pepsin, sassafras, licorice, clove, spearmint, peppermint, cinnamon, vanilla, and many kinds of fruit.

Some people like it for what it does, or what they think it does. Through the years, people have claimed that chewing gum has helped them lose weight, stop smoking, build muscles, fight boredom, play, work, and think better, stay alert, and relax. Some people claim that chewing gum helps keep their teeth clean, their breath fresh, and their mouth feeling good. And then there are the people who would not get on a plane or in a submarine without gum to help them clear their ears.

Some people buy chewing gum for the extras, such as these football cards.

Some people like what comes with it. These little extras, or novelties, have been a part of gum since it was first sold. Over the years, many different novelties have come with gum, from coupons and comics to charms and trading cards.

So what about you? Do you chew gum? What's your reason?

Facts
to Stick In your Mind

There are about 550 chewing gum companies in 93 countries around the world. Turkey has the most (about 60) followed by the United States, England, and Canada.

People in English-speaking and Latin American countries chew the most gum.

◀ The total amount of chewing gum sold in the United States in one year would make a stick 3.5 million miles (5.6 million kilometers) long. That's long enough to reach the moon and back seven times or to circle the earth 150 times at the equator.

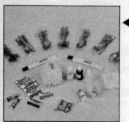

◀ Chewing gum first went into outer space on June 3, 1965. It was carried by Gemini IV astronauts James McDivett and Ed White. The gum was used to freshen their mouths after their toothbrushes were lost.

2 Chewing Gum Step-by-Step

A piece of chewing gum may be small, but it is far from simple. A lot of work goes into making that piece of gum, including special equipment, the efforts of skilled people, and ingredients from all over the world.

Chewing gum starts with a base, something to make the gum chewy. Gum base is usually a mixture of synthetic and natural materials. Synthetic base is artificially manufactured and even includes plastics made from crude oil. Natural base is made of various latexes. Latex is a milky sap, or fluid, found in trees that grow wild in rain forests around the world.

At one time, chicle was the most common

Workers at the Wrigley Chewing Gum Company wrap sticks of chewing gum.

latex used in making gum. It comes from sapodilla trees that grow in the jungles of Mexico. Chicle was a popular chewing gum ingredient until World War II, when wartime needs prevented many products from being shipped to the United States. That's when gum-makers started producing and using more synthetic bases.

Today, gum base is mainly synthetic. Some natural base is added to give the gum a smooth, even texture. However, gum-makers now use latexes such as sorva and jelutong instead of chicle. Since the supply of these latexes is more dependable than chicle, they are cheaper to buy. Sorva trees grow in the Amazon River basin, and jelutong trees grow in the rain forests of Malaysia and Indonesia.

Getting the latex from the trees isn't easy. It can only be done during the rainy season from July to December, when the latex flows the best. Workers have to find the right trees among all the

A man harvests latex from a tall, mature tree in the rain forest.

others in the rain forest. They have to make sure the tree is old enough (usually seventy years old) and has not recently been cut, since it takes the tree a number of years to build up its supply of latex. Then workers climb the trees and make zig-zag cuts using long knives called machetes. The cuts must be carefully made so that the trees are not damaged. Latex flows out of the tree, down along the cuts, and finally into a container.

The containers are collected and taken to a central camp. There the latex is strained through cloth into large kettles and boiled until it hardens. It is inspected, formed into twenty-pound rectangular blocks, and shipped to be made into chewing gum.

Chewing gum factories are filled with modern gum-making equipment. Workers in clean, white uniforms move through spotless, air-conditioned rooms overseeing the production of gum. Except for random inspection, most gum is made without ever being touched by human hands.

First, natural and synthetic gum bases are ground together into small pieces. The pieces are heated to about 240 degrees Fahrenheit (115.5 degrees Celsius) and melted into a thick syrup. The syrup is then filtered and purified before being sent to the mixers.

Chewing gum being mixed in a modern factory.

The chewing gum mixers are a lot like the mixers in your home. They are metal and have blades inside to mix ingredients. There's one difference, though, and it's a big one: chewing gum mixers are huge and can hold up to one ton of ingredients.

The ingredients for making chewing gum are added according to a formula for the gum being made. By using a formula, gum-makers can make sure each brand of gum will always taste the same.

First, sugar and corn syrup are added to the base to make the gum taste sweet and help to keep it moist. Softeners, such as vegetable oils, are then added. These help make the gum easy to chew. Finally, the flavoring is added to give the gum its taste. Some flavors are made in laboratories, while others come from plants such as spearmint or peppermint. By the time the flavor is added, the gum is no longer syrupy. It looks more like bread dough.

Only when the gum has been mixed just the right amount of time at just the right temperature does it leave the mixers. Still in big globs, it passes out of the mixers onto cooling belts. There, currents of cool air help lower its temperature. The gum then goes to machines that knead it until it is smooth. After a few hours of kneading, another machine cuts the gum into

Cooling tunnels lower the temperature of the gum so it is easier to work with.

loaf-like chunks which are easier to handle.

Some types of gum, such as soft bubble gum and ball gum, are made into a rope or pencil shape. This is done the same way you squeeze a long line of toothpaste from the tube. The gum is pushed out through a small opening, cooled, cut into chunks or balls, and wrapped.

Large sheets of chewing gum are cut into single slices by a machine.

Other types of gum are sent through a series of rollers which flatten the gum into thinner and thinner sheets. Powdered sugar is sprinkled onto the gum to keep it from sticking to the rollers and to improve the taste.

Some gum is removed while the sheets are still thick. These sheets are made into candy-coated gum and bubble gum. Other sheets are made thinner and become stick gum.

The large sheets of gum are then lightly cut into single stick sizes, but not separated. The sheets are stacked on trays and conditioned, or seasoned, for at least two days in a special room where the temperature and humidity are just right. Conditioning helps the gum stay fresh longer.

Finally, the gum is ready to be packaged. Packaging machines separate the sheets into sticks, apply the wrappers, and seal the wrapped sticks. Aluminum foil is used to keep some gum clean. Another way gum is kept clean, as well as fresh, is by putting it into airtight packages. The packaged gum is put into boxes and then shipped to stores.

But it doesn't stay there long. Soon those millions of sticks of gum are bought and chewed by people all over the world.

Facts
to Stick In your Mind

Earlier in this century, elephants were used to carry blocks of latex from the rain forests of Malaysia to its shipping ports.

More than half the weight of a piece of gum is made up of sugar. There is about one-half teaspoon of sugar in a stick of gum.

Mint is the most popular flavor for chewing gum. Mint flavor comes from the oil of mint plants. One pound of peppermint oil is enough to flavor 100 pounds (45.5 kilograms) of chewing gum.

Modern gum-wrapping machines can have up to six thousand moving parts.

The three biggest gum-makers are the William Wrigley, Jr., Company, American Chicle, and Life Savers, Inc.

3 The Roots of Chewing Gum

Chewing gum isn't new. In fact, it has its roots in early Greece. Greeks were chewing gum as early as the year A.D. 50. It wasn't the gum we chew today, but it was gum. Called *mastic*, or *mastiche* (mas·TEE·ka), it was the resin, or sap, of the mastic tree, a shrub that grows mainly in Greece and Turkey. Mastic gum is still chewed today, although beeswax is often added to soften it.

The Mayans, a Central American Indian civilization, were not far behind the Greeks. They chewed chicle, the latex of the sapodilla tree.

Native Americans in the New England area chewed the resin from the spruce tree. The Wampanoag Indians gave the Pilgrims their first taste of spruce gum in the early 1600s. When America became a nation, the custom of chewing spruce resin grew until, in the spring of 1848, the first spruce gum was manufactured for sale. It was sold by John Curtis and his son in Bradford, Maine.

Curtis's gum was made simply enough. The resin from the spruce trees was collected and boiled until it was a thick syrup. The syrup was poured onto a flat surface, rolled into sheets, and then cut into pieces. The pieces were dipped in cornstarch and wrapped in tissue paper.

Sales of the State of Maine Pure Spruce Gum were good—good enough for Curtis to hire more than 200 workers, add new brands, and spend time and money inventing gum-making machines. Sales were even good enough to build the Curtis Chewing Gum Factory, the first chewing gum factory in the world.

Spruce gum might still be popular today

Native Americans first chewed spruce resin, which led to the invention of spruce gum in the 1800s.

except for the newspaper industry. Spruce trees were needed to make newspaper. As more newspapers were sold, more spruce trees were cut down. Pretty soon there were not enough spruce trees to provide the resin for spruce gum.

But that didn't stop gum-makers. They just found something else for people to chew: paraffin, or mineral wax. The tasteless wax, made by refining crude oil, was sweetened and flavored with vanilla. Many people liked it better than spruce gum.

William F. Semple, a dentist from Mount Vernon, Ohio, had another idea for gum. He wanted it to be used for jaw exercises and gum massage. Rubber was to be the base for his gum. Semple even filed a patent on his gum in 1869, the first patent ever on a chewing gum and the process for manufacturing it. But Semple never tried to sell his gum or even make any more.

It took the help of a famous Mexican general for modern gum to come along. Antonio López de Santa Anna was well known for his victory over the Texans at the Alamo. He had also been president of Mexico before being forced to leave the country and live in exile in the United States.

Santa Anna wanted to raise an army and take over Mexico again, but for this, he needed a lot of

money. He devised a plan to raise the needed
funds. He had brought chicle with him from Mexico, and he decided to try to sell it as a rubber
substitute. It was a great plan because in the
1860s rubber was expensive and hard to get. Most
of it came from the distant rain forests of South
America and Africa.

In 1869 Santa Anna shared his idea with
Thomas Adams, Sr., a New York inventor. Adams
liked the idea and took some chicle home to
experiment with it.

Adams worked with the chicle for months,
hoping to make it into rubber. But no matter how
he refined it, chicle could not do what rubber
could. Just about the time Adams was going to
give up and throw the chicle away, something
happened. Adams was in a drugstore and saw a
little girl buy some paraffin chewing gum. He
remembered that chicle had been chewed in Mexico for many years. Adams asked the druggist if

Adams New York Chewing Gum was the first gum made from chicle sold in the United States.

he would be interested in selling another kind of gum. The druggist was, and agreed to sell Adams's new gum.

Adams went home and heated up his chicle until it was like putty. Then he rolled the chicle into little balls, wrapped them, and took them back to the druggist. The unflavored chicle gum was an instant success with the drugstore's customers.

Adams's business grew so quickly that he had to rent a building and hire twenty-five girls to wrap the gum. In 1871 he applied for and received the first patent on a gum-making machine. The machines kneaded the chicle and pushed it out in long strips that the druggist could break off into short lengths and sell for a penny each. These machines helped make it easier to manufacture and sell gum. They also helped make Adams's new business a big success.

Success didn't come so easily to the chewing gum industry, though. It took time, hard work, and several discoveries to improve chewing gum. Thomas Adams increased the appeal of gum by adding flavors. After trying sassafras, he made a licorice-flavored gum called Black Jack. Black Jack gum is still sold today, making it the oldest flavored gum on the market.

A big improvement was made in 1886, when

Licorice-flavored Black Jack gum is still sold today in many stores.

William White discovered a way to make flavors last longer. He found that mixing the flavors with corn syrup first and then adding it to the chicle base helped flavors last longer.

The creation of new bases and new flavors helped make chewing gum more popular with the public. So did the arrival of new types of gum

such as dental gum, candy-coated gum, bubble
gum, and sugarless gum.

Dentyne was the first dental gum. Invented by
Franklin V. Canning, it was first sold in 1899.
Since Dentyne had less sugar in it than other
gums, it was said to be better for people's teeth.

The idea for candy-coated gum came from
candy-coated almonds, a popular treat at the turn
of the century. Henry Fleer used that idea when
he invented the first candy-coated gum in the
early 1900s. The gum was named Chiclets, after
chicle, and is still available today.

Henry Fleer's brother Frank came up with the
first bubble gum in 1906. However, Blibber-Blubber,
as it was called, was never sold because it was too
sticky. If it stuck to your skin, the only way to get
it off was with turpentine and hard scrubbing.

It took twenty more years before a new,
improved, and less sticky bubble gum was
invented. Called Dubble Bubble, it was invented in

The name Dentyne is a combination of dental and hygiene; it was the first dental gum. Early Chiclets were flavored with creme de menthe and sold as an after-dinner treat.

1928 by Walter Diemer, an accountant for Fleer. As Diemer watched the first batch being made, he realized the gum had no color. He looked around and grabbed the only color that was there—pink! Bubble gum was a quick success, and became the largest-selling penny candy in just a few years.

Fifty years later, soft bubble gum was put on the market for people who thought the original bubble gum was too hard. Today, bubble gum comes in many shapes and sizes, from chunks to nuggets to flat slabs to long strips. It even comes coated with candy. And, because the first bubble gum was so popular, most is still colored pink.

Sugarless gum has not been available as long as many other types of gum. Sugarless gum is sweetened with chemicals instead of sugar. Without sugar, gum has fewer calories, which makes it more popular with people who are trying to lose weight. Without sugar, gum is also less likely to cause cavities.

Bubble gum comes in many shapes, such as this gum made to look like a candy apple.

This mile-long sign was one way William Wrigley, Jr., helped make his gum popular.

The first sugar-free brand, Harvey's Sugarless Gum, was introduced in the early 1950s. Shortly after that came Trident and Care Free. Today, there are many more sugarless gum brands for sale.

Along with improvements and variety, advertising was a big help to the growing gum industry.

Thomas Adams's Tutti-Fruitti gum was probably the first to be widely advertised in the late 1800s. However, William Wrigley, Jr., founder of the Wrigley Company, proved to be the leader in chewing gum advertising. He did the usual, such as placing ads in newspapers and on billboards. But he also tried new tactics, such as building a mile-long sign near Atlantic City and sending free samples to everyone in America listed in phone books.

New flavors, new gum types, and lots of advertising all helped the chewing gum industry grow. In 1914, people in the United States bought enough chewing gum for each person to have thirty-nine pieces. Now Americans buy more than six times that amount.

Facts
to Stick In your Mind

The first modern chewing gum was sold mainly in drugstores.

◀ The Wrigley Building in Chicago, Illinois, serves as the headquarters for the Wrigley Company.

The English word *masticate*, which means "to chew," comes from the Greek word *mastiche*.

Around 1900, chicle was so important in gum-making that "to chicle" meant "to chew."

William White made Yucatan, the first peppermint-flavored gum, in 1886. It was the first American brand to be popular around the world.

4 Something for Everyone

Chewing gum is popular because it has something for everyone. It wasn't always that way, though. In the days of spruce gum, all you got for your money was a small slab of gum. There were no extra flavorings, no interesting shapes, and no special bonuses.

It didn't take gum-makers long to find out what people liked. They liked their gum sweet, they liked a variety of flavors, and they liked "little extras" to come with gum.

Paraffin gum became popular in the 1850s. Not only did it come with picture cards, but it was sweetened and it came in flavors such as vanilla and licorice.

Most early chewing gums were flavored with mint. Later, fruit flavors became popular.

More flavors were added to gum in the late 1800s. Most were developed by druggists, since they could easily get flavorings and they knew how to mix them. Some of the most popular were fruit and peppermint.

Many more flavors have been used over the years. Spearmint and peppermint have been favorites, as have wintergreen, grape, cinnamon, sassafras, and clove.

Today, almost any kind of flavor is available. You can buy fruit flavors such as strawberry, blueberry, raspberry, orange, lemon, lime, banana, cherry, apple, and watermelon. Soft-drink flavors of gum such as cola and Dr. Pepper are also available. You can even buy chocolate mint-flavored gum.

Flavors aren't the only reason people chew gum. Many people like the different forms gum comes in. Over the years, gum-makers have introduced new shapes. First there was the slab of spruce gum, followed by the stick, and the chunk of bubble gum.

And then there were gumballs. Billions have been chewed since their creation in the early 1900s. The reasons are simple: gumballs are easy to get and they are cheap. You can find gumball machines almost anywhere, and you can still buy a gumball for a penny. Besides, a shiny bright ball of gum can be made to look like a number of interesting things, from snowballs to satellites.

Shaping gum into slabs, sticks, chunks, and balls was only the beginning. Today, gum can be molded into just about any shape. That's why you'll find gum in the shapes of hot dogs, hamburgers, french fries, cheese, and even pizza. Add to those the shapes that paraffin gum comes in: whistles, lips, mustaches, and don't forget buck teeth, horse teeth, and fangs.

Some people don't even care how gum looks or what it tastes like. They buy gum for the things

Gumball machines can be found almost anywhere, and gumballs still cost only one penny.

that come with it. The picture cards that first
came with paraffin gum in the 1800s were only the
beginning of a long tradition. Over the years, trading cards have featured TV characters, movie
stars, war heroes, rock 'n roll stars, political can-
didates, and sports figures.

The most popular trading cards of all time
have been baseball cards. However, the first
baseball cards did not come with gum; they came
in packs of cigarettes beginning in 1886. During
the 1930s, baseball cards started coming with
gum, and since that time, many billions have been
sold. Today, baseball cards are the focus of
books, businesses, and even conventions.

Comics have been another reason for buying
gum. They were started by the Fleer Corporation,
makers of Dubble Bubble, to help make their gum
special when so many other companies started
manufacturing bubble gum. Other companies
added comics, and now they are made in more

An early baseball card from a package of chewing gum.

than fifty different languages for distribution all over the world.

For people not excited about trading cards or comics, other things have come with gum over the years. Charms, stickers, horoscopes, stamps, miniature statues, jokes, tattoos, and premiums have been used.

Today, baseball cards from gum packages are traded by children and adults.

The Wrigley Company was offering premiums, or prizes, even before 1900. Wholesalers, retailers, and gum-buyers received coupons to trade for premiums. Items offered included lamps, clocks, flags, and cash registers. New inventions such as fountain pens, safety razors, and cameras were also offered. By the 1950s, though, premiums became too costly and were no longer offered by the Wrigley Company. Today, however, some gum-makers still include coupons for prizes with their gum.

Sometimes people buy gum so they can help others. One gum company, the Ford Gum & Machine Company, set up a program in 1939 to help raise money for charity. The program was simple: Ford provided the gumball machines, and the charity organization received a part of the profits from gumball sales. Today, Ford helps raise more than two million dollars a year for more than six thousand local service clubs and charities.

Ford gumball machines provide money for charity.

Gum comes with a lot of appealing extras. Still, fancy flavors, shapes, and novelties are not the only things to consider before deciding whether or not to chew gum. There are some surprising things you should know about chewing gum and your health.

Facts
to Stick In your Mind

Some comics don't come with words. They are done in pictures for use in countries in Africa as well as in the Near East, Far East, and Asia.

Baseball players each make between $250 and $500 plus a yearly royalty for use of their pictures on baseball cards.

Susan Montgomery Williams, of Fresno, California, has blown the biggest bubble on record. On April 19, 1985, she blew a bubble that measured 22 inches (56 centimeters) in diameter. Her record is listed in the *Guinness Book of World Records*.

The largest piece of bubble gum ever made came from the Topps Chewing Gum Company. It was as big and as heavy as ten thousand regular pieces of Topps bubble gum and was presented to baseball player Willie Mays in June 1974.

5 To Chew or Not to Chew

Over the years there have been many arguments both for and against chewing gum. They can be narrowed down to one basic question: is it healthy to chew gum? To answer this question, let's begin by looking at what gum does to your teeth. First, you should know what cavities are and how they are formed.

Cavities are small holes in your teeth which are caused by acid made by the bacteria in your mouth. Your mouth is filled with these tiny living creatures. When bacteria break down food—especially foods that have sugar in them—acid is produced. This acid is strong enough to eventually make a hole in a tooth.

Things get worse when you don't brush and floss your teeth, because then you don't get the bacteria off of your teeth. That means when acid is made, it is in direct contact with your teeth and can work faster.

So what happens when you chew gum sweetened with sugar? It may seem that the sugar would cause more acid, which would make more cavities. However, chewing gum causes the salivary glands to make more saliva—not a little bit more, either, but more than 250 percent more. The saliva helps wash small pieces of food from your mouth to your stomach. It also washes the sugar from the gum into your stomach in about two to three minutes. In addition, the saliva helps to neutralize the acid in your mouth so that it is not so strong.

So, the sugar in chewing gum helps bacteria produce more of the acid that can cause cavities. But chewing the gum helps your mouth produce more saliva, which reduces the damage the acid will do to your teeth. That makes it better than eating other kinds of snacks flavored with sugar.

Sugarless gum is better for your teeth because it brings more saliva to your mouth without adding any sugar. Tests have proven that sugarless gum does not cause cavities, and can actually prevent cavities from getting bigger. Chewing it after a sweet snack is helpful when you can't brush your teeth.

Sugarless gum may be better for your teeth, but it might cause other problems. In the past, chemicals such as cyclamate and saccharin were used to replace sugar in gum. After testing, cyclamate was found to cause cancer in laboratory animals. The evidence against saccharin was not as strong. It can be used, but products containing saccharin must have a warning label. Aspartame is another artificial sweetener used today. It was tested for more than ten years before it was determined to be safe. Still, some people think aspartame was put on the market too soon, and that more tests need to be done.

Gum has been accused of worse things than causing cavities. People have blamed chewing gum for spreading colds and flu. And they're right, gum can spread colds and flu. However, it is not the fault of gum-makers, but the people who chew it.

Some people share their gum. If you share gum you have already been chewing, you are sharing more than your gum. You are also sharing your germs. And then there are the people who like to take the gum from their mouths and put it somewhere while they do something else. When they pick up their gum, they're also picking up the germs that were on the place their gum was "parked."

Although some believe that bubble gum causes crooked teeth or buck teeth, there is no

proof to support this claim. Nor is there proof
that gum can help whiten teeth. But gum can help
sweeten your breath, and the chewing action is
good for your gums because it helps the blood
circulate.

In the early days of chewing gum, some people claimed gum was made from horse hooves
and glue. If you swallowed it, they said, it would
plug your intestines.

Actually, swallowing gum is almost always
harmless. Still, there is at least one rare case that
had to do with a two-year-old girl. She was rushed
to the hospital one night with a painfully puffed-up
stomach. The doctor soon found the problem:
something was blocking the girl's intestines. When
the blockage was taken out, it turned out to be a
3.57-ounce chuck of bubble gum. That's about ten
pieces!

Some people get stomachaches when they
chew a lot of sugarless gum that is sweetened

with sorbitol. Stomachaches occur because sorbitol cannot be digested. Instead, it ferments in
your digestive system, which can cause upset
stomachs as well as diarrhea.

Stomachaches can also be caused by swallowing unchewed food. According to one popular
belief, if you chew lots of gum, your jaws get too
tired to chew your food properly.

While this is possible, it is more likely that
your jaws would be too tired to chew anything.
For example, a marine, who later became a dentist, was serving on an island in the Pacific Ocean
during World War II. When he and a buddy found
a case of chewing gum, they decided to see who
could chew the most. After putting twenty-seven
sticks of gum into each of their mouths, neither
was interested in the contest. In fact, their jaw
muscles were so sore they weren't interested in
eating for three days!

People who have just had their tonsils taken

out are usually not interested in eating, either. Their throats are sore for a few days after the operation. But gum can help them. Doctors have found that bubble gum is especially good because it helps the salivary glands produce more saliva, which makes it easier to swallow and helps ease the pain until the throat heals.

Increasing saliva also causes people to swallow more frequently. Gum can be very helpful when your ears are blocked with a cold or when you're up in an airplane. Swallowing helps open your eustachian tube, which runs from your middle ear to the back of your throat. This tube is important because it makes the air pressure equal between your middle ear and the outside world. Swallowing helps it do its job.

Gum has often helped people who try to kick bad habits. One habit that many people try to break is overeating. For some dieters, chewing gum takes the place of eating something that would be more fattening. For others, though, chewing gum makes them more hungry.

Smoking is another habit people try to break with the help of gum. Doctors can prescribe a special gum with nicotine in it to help break the smoking habit. Nicotine is an addictive drug that is in tobacco. By chewing nicotine gum, which contains less nicotine than tobacco does, people can cut down on the drug until they no longer need it at all.

Studies done as early as the 1930s show that chewing gum can help people feel more at ease. Chewing helps lower muscle tension and makes it easier to relax. The chewing action can also replace nervous habits. Scientists have found that when people chew gum, they drop nervous habits such as twitching or tapping. Although a person can chew just about anything to feel less tense, gum is often one of the easiest and most convenient things to chew.

Chewing gum will also help you stay awake and alert. That's why the Armed Forces have supplied soldiers with gum since the days of World War I.

So, is gum a health food or is it a junk food? It's neither. While it might help you stay calm, it won't make you any healthier. Yet, unless you're a very rare case, it won't really hurt you, either.

While sugarless gum is a healthier choice, there are no strong health reasons to chew or not to chew gum. That means you have to use other personal reasons to decide whether to chew gum. If it looks good, tastes good, and the price seems right, go ahead and chew.

Facts
to Stick In your Mind

◄ In the 1920s, heavyweight boxing champion Jack Dempsey chewed gum to make his jaw stronger. It worked. One opponent, Georges Carpentier, broke his thumb when he hit Dempsey in the jaw.

There are ten calories in a stick of gum, seven calories in a stick of sugarless gum, and about twenty calories in a piece of bubble gum.

Swallowed gum takes from one to three days to pass through your digestive system. Unlike other food, it stays in one piece because the gum base cannot be digested.

◄ The explorer Admiral Richard Byrd carried gum with him on his expedition to Antarctica in order to calm his nerves.

6 A Final Taste

You have read a lot about chewing gum, but you may still have some questions, such as these.

Question: Do people buy about the same amount of gum each year?

Answer: Not at all. Chewing gum sales go down during calm times and up during tense times. That's why gum sales were high during World War I, Prohibition (when alcohol was illegal), and in 1964 when the Surgeon General warned that smoking causes cancer.

Question: Is it considered polite to chew gum?

Answer: Most books on etiquette, or manners, consider gum to be a bad habit and believe that it

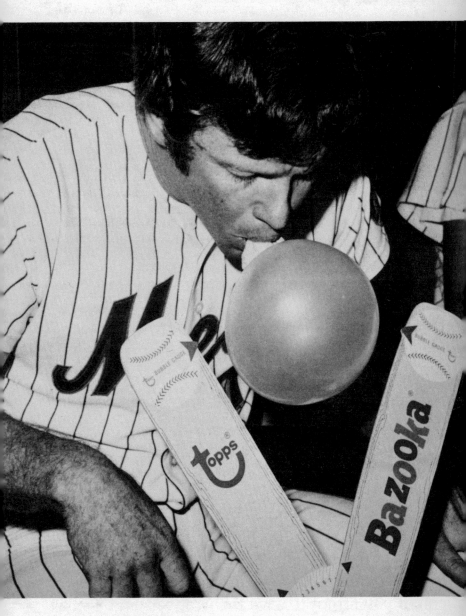

A "bubble gauge" measures the size of the bubble this baseball player has blown.

shouldn't be chewed at all, much less in public.
Yet millions of people don't take that advice. If
you are one of them, you can still be considerate
by chewing gum quietly around others. Save your
noisy chewing, gum cracking, and bubble blowing
for times when you're alone.

Question: What is the polite way to get rid of
chewed gum?

Answer: Well, it's definitely not polite to spit it
out on the sidewalk or stick it under your seat.
You would know that if you ever got gum stuck to
your shoes or clothing. The best way to get rid of
your gum is to plan ahead just a little. When you
unwrap the gum to put it in your mouth, keep the
wrapper. Then, when you're done chewing, simply
put the wrapper up to your mouth and take out
the piece of gum with it. Make sure the gum is
totally wrapped and then throw it in a garbage
can. If you forgot to save the wrapper, find a small

piece of paper to wrap your gum in before throwing it away.

Question: How can you get chewed gum off of things?

Answer: That depends on what it's stuck to. If a big bubble pops and sticks to your face, use the rest of the gum to get it off. It will come off easily by taking the gum from your mouth and dabbing it at the gum stuck to your face.

If there's gum stuck to clothing, fabric, or furniture, rub an ice cube over the gum. When the gum hardens and starts to crumble, gently scrape it off with a knife. If the gum is stuck to a small piece of clothing or fabric, place the object in a plastic bag and put it in the freezer. When the gum is frozen, it will come off with a flick of your finger.

If gum is stuck in your hair, peanut butter is the answer. Take a little dab and rub it into your

Baseball players take part in a bubble-blowing contest to promote their baseball cards.

hair where the gum is. The oil in the peanut butter will loosen the gum so you can pull it right out.

Question: Why is it easier to blow bubbles with some kinds of gum?

Answer: The base for bubble gum is different

than the base for other types of gum. Since gum formulas are considered top secret by gummakers, we do not know exactly how they are different. But we do know that bubble gum base is better able to stretch and, at the same time, hold together. That makes it easier to blow bubbles.

Question: What do people in other countries call gum?

Answer: People in many Latin American countries call it *goma de mascar*. Arabs call it *elki*. The Germans and Austrians call it *kaugummi*. The Chinese call it *heung how chu*. The Greeks call it *tsikles*. The Japanese call it *gamu*. The Norwegians call it *tyggegummi*. The Portuguese call it *pastilka elastica*. The Russians call it *zhevatelnaya rezinka*. The Swedish call it *tuggumi*. The Swiss call it *chaetschgummi*.

Question: Has gum been used for things other than chewing?

Answer: Gum has been used for many things over the years. During the hard times of the Great Depression, gum was used to "fish" for coins. A chewed piece of gum was stuck to a stone that was tied to a long string. The string was lowered through gratings on the sidewalk where coins had been dropped. The coins would stick to the gum and then be pulled up.

Gum has been used by gardeners, too. Some gardeners who don't like to use chemicals to kill bugs use liquid bubble gum instead. Bugs are attracted to the bubble gum and try to eat it. But when they do, their jaws stick shut, making garden plants safe from their bites.

Gum has even inspired a dance and a work of art. Chicagoan Linda Martha has created a modern dance called *Sticks of It*. It is made up of several dance scenes with titles such as "Sugarless," "Double Mint," "Big Red," "Juicy Fruit," and "Bubble Gum Boogie." *Sticks of It* has

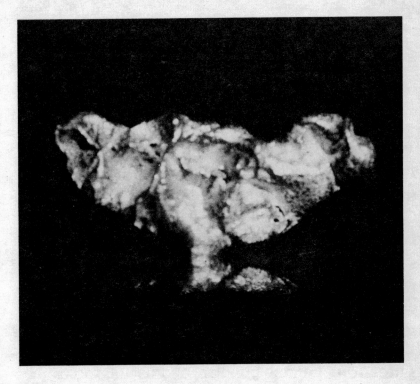

One of Les Levine's gum sculptures.

been performed in Eugene, Oregon, as well as in Chicago.

Les Levine, a New York artist, created a series of chewing gum sculptures in the early 1970s. First, he chewed thirty pieces of Double-mint gum for exactly two minutes each. Then he sent the pieces to be cast in eighteen-carat gold.

He mounted each piece on a pin, which holds the gold gum to a black marble base.

Levine's gum sculpture has been popular. It has been shown in some of the most famous art galleries around the world, including the Fischbach Gallery and the Museum of Modern Art in New York City, and the Jollenbeck Galerie in West Germany.

Question: Gum is popular, and useful, too. But has it ever done anything really important?

Answer: For one thing, gum has helped solve crimes. Dr. William Alexander, a dentist from Oregon, has used gum to help catch criminals. In one murder case, a suspect claimed he was not at the scene of the crime. Dr. Alexander proved otherwise. Chewed gum had been found at the scene by a police officer. From the saliva on the gum, Dr. Alexander was able to find out the chewer's blood type. It was the same as the

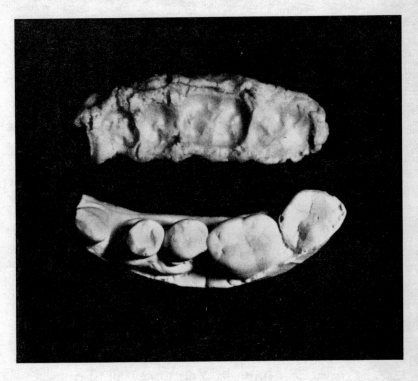

Teeth imprints on chewed gum have been used to solve crimes.

suspect's. Dr. Alexander then took an impression of the suspect's mouth and compared it with the bite marks on the gum. They were exactly the same. The suspect was arrested and found guilty.

Gum has also helped save lives. In 1911, a British Royal Air Force dirigible, a blimplike airship, was making a flight to the United States.

Halfway across the Atlantic, the crew found a leak
in the water jacket of the engine. To keep from
crashing into the ocean, they had to fix that leak
quickly. The crew tried everything to fix the leak,
but nothing worked. As a last hope, gum was
passed out to the crew. The chewed gum was put
together and plastered on the leak. It worked!
Thanks to chewing gum, the crew lived to tell
about their frightening experience.

So, now you have it. You know all about
chewing gum: its long and interesting history,
what is in it, how it is made, and what it can and
cannot do for you. And you know how popular
gum is. All these things should give you something
to think about the next time you pop a piece of
chewing gum into your mouth.

Happy chewing!

Time
LINE

A.D. 50	Greeks chew mastiche, a resin from the mastic tree
A.D. 200	Mayans chew chicle, a resin from the sapodilla tree
A.D. 200	North American Indians chew spruce resin
Early 1600s	Wampanoag Indians introduce Pilgrims to spruce gum
1848	John Curtis of Bradford, Maine, makes the first commercial spruce gum
1850	Curtis begins making paraffin gum
1869	William F. Semple, a dentist from Mt. Vernon, Ohio, is the first to patent a chewing gum; he uses rubber as his base
1869	General Antonio López de Santa Anna sells chicle to Thomas Adams, Sr.; Adams makes the first commercial chicle gum
1870	Adams makes Black Jack, the first mass-produced, flavored gum
1871	Adams patents the first gum-making machine
1886	William White finds a way to make flavors last longer in gum
1892	William Wrigley, Jr., baking powder salesman, offers chewing gum as a premium

1893   Wrigley enters the gum-making business; Wrigley's Spearmint and Juicy Fruit are first sold

1899   Franklin V. Channing invents Dentyne, the first dental gum

Approx. 1900   Henry Fleer invents Chiclets, the first candy-coated gum

Early 1900s   Gumballs are first offered for sale

1906   Blibber-Blubber, the first bubble gum, is invented; it is too sticky to sell

1915   Wrigley's sends gum samples to everyone listed in U.S. telephone books

1928   Walter Diemer, an accountant at Fleer, invents Dubble Bubble; it is the first bubble gum ever sold

1939   Ford Gum & Machine Company sets up a gumball sales program to help charities

Early 1950s   Sugarless gum comes onto the market

1965   Gemini IV astronauts carry gum into space for the first time

1974   Bubble Yum, the first soft bubble gum, is introduced by Life Savers, Inc.

1985   Susan Montgomery Williams blows a twenty-two-inch bubble, the biggest on record

Index